NAVY SEALS

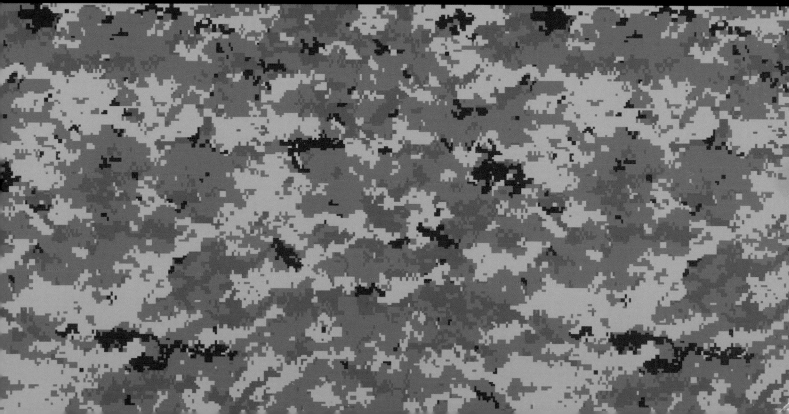

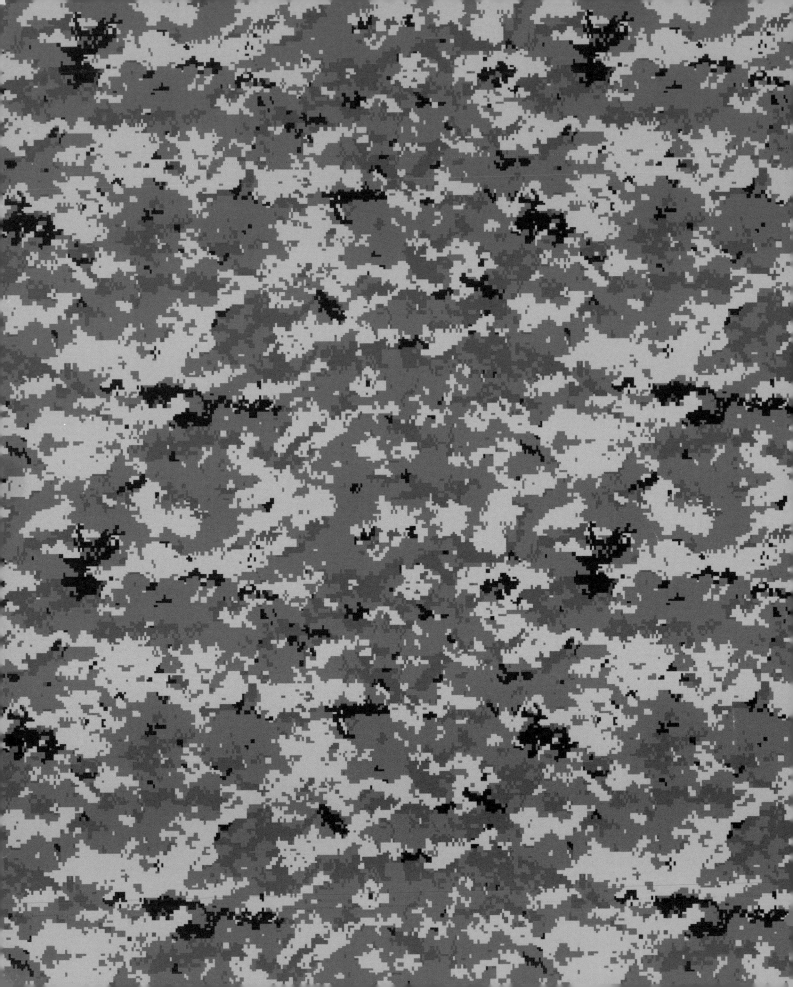

U.S. SPECIAL FORCES

NAVY SEALS

JIM WHITING

PUBLISHED BY Creative Paperbacks

P.O. Box 227, Mankato, Minnesota 56002

Creative Paperbacks is an imprint of The Creative Company

www.thecreativecompany.us

DESIGN AND PRODUCTION BY Christine Vanderbeek

ART DIRECTION BY Rita Marshall

PRINTED IN the United States of America

PHOTOGRAPHS BY

Alamy (AF archive, Pictorial Press Ltd, RGB Ventures LLC dba
SuperStock, United Archives GmbH, US Navy Photo), Corbis
(CORBIS, epa, Lance Iversen/San Francisco Chronicle, Karen
Kasmauski, Sebastian Rich, Louie Psihoyos, Shepard Sherbell,
AKHTAR SOOMRO/Reuters, Stocktrek Images), Getty Images
(Lisa Pembleton, U.S. Navy/Authenticated News), iStockphoto
(spxChrome), Shutterstock (ALMAGAMI, gst), SuperStock
(Stocktrek Images, U.S. Navy Public Domain/Science Faction)

LIBRARY OF CONGRESS CATALOGING-IN-PUBLICATION DATA

Whiting, Jim.

Navy SEALs / Jim Whiting.

p. cm. — (U.S. Special Forces)

Includes bibliographical references and index.

Summary: A chronological account of the American special forces
unit known as the Navy SEALs, including key details about important
figures, landmark missions, and controversies.

ISBN 978-1-60818-465-1 (HARDCOVER)

ISBN 978-1-62832-051-0 (PBK)

1. United States. Navy. SEALs—Juvenile literature. 2. United States.
Navy—Commando troops—Juvenile literature. I. Title.

VG87.W54 2014

359.9'84—dc23   2013036211

CCSS: RI.5.1, 2, 3, 8; RH.6-8.4, 5, 6, 8

FIRST EDITION

9 8 7 6 5 4 3 2 1

U.S. SPECIAL FORCES

TABLE OF CONTENTS

★ ★ ★

A SEAL's training in combat diving makes him as formidable off land as on.

FORCE FACTS Jacques Cousteau made significant improvements to earlier diving technologies during the 1940s and is generally regarded as the father of modern scuba diving.

INTRODUCTION

SHORTLY AFTER MIDNIGHT ON MAY 2, 2011, SOHAIB ATHAR heard a loud clattering near his home in Abbottabad, Pakistan. "Helicopter hovering above Abbottabad," he tweeted to his followers. A few minutes later he added, "A huge window shaking bang."

Athar was witnessing the culmination of an exhausting 10-year search for al Qaeda terrorist and 9/11 mastermind Osama bin Laden. American intelligence authorities believed they had finally located him in a high-walled compound in Abbottabad. United States president Barack Obama decided that a raid was the best way of capturing or killing him. For this task, he chose a squadron from one of America's elite special operations forces (SOFs): the Naval Special Warfare Development Group, or DEVGRU, more commonly known as SEAL Team Six.

After several weeks of preparation, everything was finally ready. Two Black Hawk helicopters flown by the 160th Special Operations Aviation Regiment (Airborne) took off from a base in Afghanistan near the Pakistani border. They carried 24 SEALs and a combat dog. Several other choppers were on high alert to provide backup, if necessary. The operation was kept secret from the Pakistani government for fear that someone would tip off bin Laden.

During the 90-minute flight, the helicopter pilots hugged the contours of the ground to avoid radar detection. Planners had taken great pains to come up with the most effective strategy. But they hadn't accounted for one thing. When one of the helicopters began its descent over the compound, the high walls kept the *downwash* from the rotors from properly diffusing. The copter rapidly lost altitude. Moments later, it crashed....

The Abbottabad compound kept Osama bin Laden hidden from the public for years.

ACTIVE IN ALL ENVIRONMENTS

SEALs ARE THE U.S. NAVY'S SPECIAL OPERATIONS FORCE. The term is an *acronym* for Sea, Air, and Land, indicating the three operational environments of its members. SEALs fall under the administration of the U.S. Special Operations Command (SOCOM) and are one of America's primary weapons in the global fight against terrorism.

Warriors similar to SEALs go back many centuries. During the period of the Byzantine Empire (330–1453), men would sometimes swim out to enemy warships at night to cut the anchor chains, setting the vessels adrift. They had to hold their breath for several minutes and had only primitive tools to perform their missions. At other times, the Byzantines used small, fast-moving ships to scout out enemy forces and launch lightning-fast, commando-style raids. They frequently were in conflict with Muslim forces, who adopted similarly covert, or secretive, tactics against them and other Christian forces. During the period of the *Crusades*, Muslim soldiers would disguise themselves and their ships, and then pull alongside Crusader vessels and swarm aboard to kill their enemies.

In the 1940s, American forces needed to scout out potential obstacles before landing on the beaches of Japanese-held islands in the Pacific Ocean. In August 1942, volunteers from the army and navy known as the Scouts and Raiders gathered at the Amphibious Training Base in Little Creek, Virginia. Within two months, they were on their way to North Africa to support the *Allied* offensive known as Operation Torch. At first, the Scouts and Raiders carried out their dangerous missions armed with little more than a K-Bar knife, giving them the nickname "naked

SEALs skillfully operate in shallow waters unreachable by ships and submarines.

FORCE FACTS When World War II ended in 1945, just four UDT teams—two on each coast comprising a total of 7 officers and 45 *enlisted men*—remained on active duty.

warriors." Later, their training in blowing up obstacles led to their becoming known as Underwater Demolition Teams (UDTs). Eventually, 34 UDTs were established and dispersed around the globe. They often faced highly volatile conditions, with the largest loss of life involving UDT personnel occurring on June 6, 1944. More than 90 UDT members were killed or wounded as they opened gaps in the German shore defenses during the D-Day landings in Normandy, France. When the war ended, most of the men were discharged from UDTs.

The onset of the Korean War in 1950 led to a renewed interest in underwater activity. By then, breakthroughs in breathing technology greatly enhanced the scope of action for the UDTs, who used scuba gear for the first time. They also expanded their range of operations beyond *reconnaissance* and beach clearance, attacking supply lines located further inland.

In May 1961, four months after assuming the presidency, John F. Kennedy made a high-profile speech in which he committed the U.S. to putting a man on the moon by the end of the decade. While it wasn't as dramatic or as newsworthy, in the same speech, the president laid out a plan to develop more SOFs to help the existing Army Special Forces (Green Berets) and Air Force Special Commandos in combatting communist-backed *guerrilla* activity—so-called "wars of national liberation"—in many countries. Kennedy, a World War II naval hero, was especially interested in developing a seaborne special forces component. As a result, SEAL Teams 1 and 2 were officially formed on January 1, 1962, and operated throughout the Vietnam War. But as had happened following World War II, SOF numbers were cut substantially when the Vietnam conflict ended in the mid-1970s. Conventional military leaders believed not only that all special forces received too much fame and publicity but also that they had no role to play in the ongoing conflict with the Soviet Union.

As the nature of warfare changed, such thinking became

As predecessors to SEALs, UDT operators cleared beaches before amphibious landings.

FORCE FACTS The only publicly identified SEAL on the bin Laden raid was a dog named Cairo. Public interest in adopting retired military dogs spiked when his name was released.

outmoded, and SEALs increasingly proved their worth. They participated in Operation Urgent Fury on the Caribbean island of Grenada in 1983 and in Operation Just Cause, the invasion of Panama, six years later. But their real value became evident in the turmoil in the Middle East that began in the early 1990s. The scope of SEAL missions widened further in the wake of the 9/11 terrorist attacks in 2001 as SEALs became essential during the wars in Afghanistan and Iraq. Former SEAL Dick Couch notes, "SEALs, with their highly trained, disciplined strike teams, quickly became the [special operations] force of choice for rapid-response direct-action missions.... Team leaders would often brief their men en route—on the way to the target. They quickly became adept at hitting the ground running and shooting."

As demands for their services have increased in recent years, so have their numbers. Today, there are eight active teams, in addition to SEAL Team Six. Teams 1, 3, 5, and 7 comprise Naval Special Warfare Group 1, which is based in Coronado, California, while Teams 2, 4, 8, and 10 form the Naval Special Warfare Group 2. Their base is in Little Creek, Virginia. Each team consists of 8 operational 16-man platoons, with 2 officers and 14 enlisted men. Each platoon can be broken down into two squads of eight men, with four-man fire teams (three riflemen and a machine gunner) or even two-man sniper/reconnaissance teams.

Recent high-profile operations—such as the bin Laden raid—have returned SEAL Team Six to the spotlight and caused people to wonder more about its history and inner workings. The origins of Team Six date back to the failure of Operation Eagle Claw, a 1980 mission to rescue several dozen American hostages in Iran who had been captured the previous

Bin Laden called for the destruction of all who stood in the way of his radical ideal of Islam.

year. Despite careful planning, the mission failed. The failure pointed out the need for a joint command that cut across individual service lines. Lieutenant Commander Richard Marcinko, a highly decorated SEAL during the Vietnam War, insisted on the formation of an elite SEAL team devoted primarily to counterterrorism that would become part of this new command. He became its first commander. "I called the unit SEAL Team Six," he explained. "Six because there were already six platoons [among existing SEAL teams] that had received CT [counterterrorist] training. And six because the number would make the Soviets believe that there were five other SEAL teams somewhere, when there were in fact only two." Marcinko began with 15 officers and 75 enlisted men, putting them through an intense 6-month training course. Traditional navy grooming standards gave way to long hair, beards, and mustaches so that the men could appear to be civilians. Marcinko also emphasized language skills.

The unit was officially disbanded in 1987 and replaced by the highly secretive DEVGRU, though the original name is often used instead. There is considerable evidence that DEVGRU's core

SEALs and other forces from the U.S. and Caribbean invaded Grenada to help restore order.

missions remained almost unchanged and that many of the team's original members were retained in the new organization. While considerably less remains officially known about SEAL Team Six than the other teams, it appears that the unit is divided into 4 assault team squadrons—Red, Blue, Silver, and Gold—each of which has about 50 men. The squadrons are divided into three troops, which in turn are divided into teams of assaulters and snipers. In addition to the assault teams are Black Squadron, which carries out reconnaissance and surveillance, and Gray Squadron, consisting of boat crews that deliver the men to their objectives. Finally, Green Team is the name given to the training unit.

Navy SEALs are sometimes tasked with destroying stockpiles of ammunition and supplies.

FORCE FACTS During its initial training, SEAL Team Six became so good at mountaineering that when the men checked into a hotel, they sometimes climbed the outside of the building to reach their rooms.

EARNING THE TRIDENT

PROSPECTIVE ENLISTED SEALs ARE RECRUITED FROM WITH-in the armed forces or outside it. They must undergo a battery of tests that measure their intelligence, ability to learn, and mental toughness. They must also pass the minimum standards of the 5-part Physical Screening Test (PST), being able to swim 500 yards (457 m) in 12.5 minutes, do 42 pushups in 2 minutes, 50 sit-ups in 2 minutes, 6 pull-ups, and run 1.5 miles (2.4 km) in 11 minutes while wearing combat boots. As former SEAL Howard Wasdin explains, "Each activity by itself wasn't so difficult, but doing one after the other was." Only half the men in his group passed the PST.

Because there are only a limited number of commissioned officers in the SEAL program, competition for the available slots is intense. Most of these applicants are already naval officers, though some graduating Naval Academy *cadets* and a few officers from other services also seek admittance. A successful candidate will demonstrate superior leadership skills, outstanding academic performance, cultural and language aptitude, and high achievement in competitive sports. PST scores are especially important.

Being accepted as a prospective SEAL is just the beginning. Candidates soon enter Basic Underwater Demolition/SEAL training (BUD/S), which lasts for more than seven months. It begins with a five-week *indoctrination* session at the Naval Special Warfare Preparatory School in Great Lakes, Illinois. That session

In a BUD/S drill called "the sugar cookie," wet recruits roll in the sand and perform pushups.

ends with an intensified version of the PST. Now the men must swim 1,000 yards (914 m) in 20 minutes, do 70 pushups in 2 minutes, 60 sit-ups in 2 minutes, 10 pull-ups, and run 4 miles (6.4 km) in 31 minutes. Successful passage leads to actual BUD/S training at the Naval Special Warfare Center in Coronado, California. It consists of three phases.

The first phase emphasizes physical conditioning and also lays the groundwork for the team-building so important for SEALs to have. For seven weeks, candidates endure a rigorous regimen of steadily increasing amounts of running, calisthenics, and swimming as well as such exercises as manipulating heavy logs the size of telephone poles. Each week they face timed four-mile (6.4 km) runs, two-mile (3.2 km) swims, and an obstacle course, and they are expected to improve each time. While some of the swimming takes place in pools, most is in the Pacific Ocean, where the water temperature ranges from 72 °F (22 °C) in August to a bone-chilling 59 °F (15 °C) in January. It's not uncommon for trainees to become somewhat *hypothermic* during some of their longer swims, which may last for several hours.

Hell Week—one of the most grueling and demanding aspects of training that any military force in the world undergoes—comes midway through phase one. For 5.5 days, the men do physical training for more than 20 hours a day. By the time it is over, they have run more than 200 miles (320 km)—nearly 8 full marathons—and swum countless miles in the ocean. One of the aims of Hell Week is to push candidates to their limits and beyond. They endure harsh physical conditions meant to replicate the extreme stresses of battle and are granted only four hours of sleep during the entire week. "Successful completion of Hell Week truly defines those candidates who have the commitment and dedication required of a SEAL," notes the official SEAL website. Mark Owen, who took part in the bin Laden raid, says, "I'd made it through ... BUD/S by focusing on just making it

Exhausted SEALs work as a team to move logs weighing 300 pounds (136 kg) during Hell Week.

to the next meal. It didn't matter if I couldn't feel my arms as we hoisted logs over our heads or if the cold surf soaked me to the core. It wasn't going to last forever."

The second BUD/S phase teaches the candidates to become combat-ready scuba divers in seven weeks. Trainees learn a variety of techniques involving underwater breathing apparatuses and become comfortable in a marine environment. Night diving is necessary to achieve this comfort level, since so many SEAL operations take place under the cover of darkness.

The third and final training phase lasts for nine weeks and emphasizes demolition and *small-unit tactics*. Physical training intensifies, with running distances increasing and the pace per mile decreasing. The same holds true for swimming and the obstacle course. At the same time, the men learn land navigation, reconnaissance techniques, rappelling, demolitions, and more. The final four weeks of this phase take place at the Maritime Operations Facility on San Clemente Island. There, the men conduct practice missions that allow them to use their recently gained knowledge in conditions as close as possible to what they are likely to face in real life.

Typically, just one in every five men who began training will make it this far. Even after graduating from BUD/s, a SEAL's training is far from over. The next stage is airborne school, for three weeks of intensive parachute training. Then they return to the Naval Special Warfare Center for more than four months of SEAL Qualification Training (SQT). This involves honing their skills in weapons training, working closely with unit members, treating battlefield wounds, and familiarizing themselves with extreme climate conditions. They visit a cold-weather site such as Kodiak, Alaska, to learn how to deal with water temperatures

Instructors check the recruits' underwater knots and communicate through hand signals.

just above freezing. Then they go to Camp Billy Machen (named for the first SEAL to die in Vietnam) in the California high desert for live-fire exercises involving small arms, shoulder-launched rockets, and explosive charges. The final step is the Survival, Evasion, Resistance, and Escape (SERE) course, which teaches techniques of avoiding and enduring capture.

After completion of SERE, newly minted SEALs receive the coveted trident insignia and are assigned to a team. Many of them take additional advanced courses, such as sniper school or intensive language education. They also spend months training with their team prior to *deployment*. Ideally, each team has a six-month deployment every two years and spends the remaining time honing their training. In recent years, however, deployments have often occurred with greater frequency.

At some point, many SEALs want to join Team Six because they regard it as the highest level of their chosen field. As Wasdin, who became a SEAL in the late 1980s and later joined Team Six, wrote, "When the U.S. Navy sends their elite, they send the SEALs. When the SEALs send their elite, they send SEAL Team

BUD/S candidates undergo cold-water conditioning, or "surf torture," between fitness drills.

Six.... Its job is to fight terrorism and armed rebellion, often secretly."

The secrecy surrounding Team Six extends to its processes of selection and training, though it appears that all applicants come from existing SEAL teams and undergo an advanced training course that lasts nine months. Its motto is "the more you sweat in peace, the less you'll bleed in war." Even getting in is rigorous. According to some sources, applicants' photos are posted in the team's headquarters in Dam Neck, Virginia—not far from Little Creek—and current members indicate their approval or disapproval. Others say that candidates may face a grim, unsmiling board of selection composed of Team Six members.

Once admitted to Team Six, the training is even more strenuous than traditional SEAL training. Wasdin said he made more than 150 parachute jumps in 4 weeks—many of them from high altitudes, with others involving "stacking," a procedure in which all the men are aligned vertically—an average of nearly 6 jumps a day. They also shoot, shoot, and keep shooting. "We shot thousands of rounds every day," Wasdin continued. "I was told that in one year, SEAL Team Six alone spent more money just on 9 mm ammunition than the entire Marine Corps spent on all its ammunition." Much of this shooting takes place in advanced levels of close quarters combat (CQC) under the watchful eyes of instructors who continually reconfigure the confined training spaces and videotape the encounters to provide immediate feedback. The realistic training conditions can sometimes result in accidents that cause severe wounds and even death.

SEALs must safely navigate all types of water bodies, including rivers, swamps, and oceans.

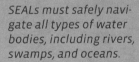

FORCE FACTS Many SEALs arrive at their targets in rigid-hull inflatable boats (RHIBs), which are 36 feet (11 m) long, 10.5 feet (3.2 m) wide, and have a top of speed of more than 40 nautical miles (74 km) per hour.

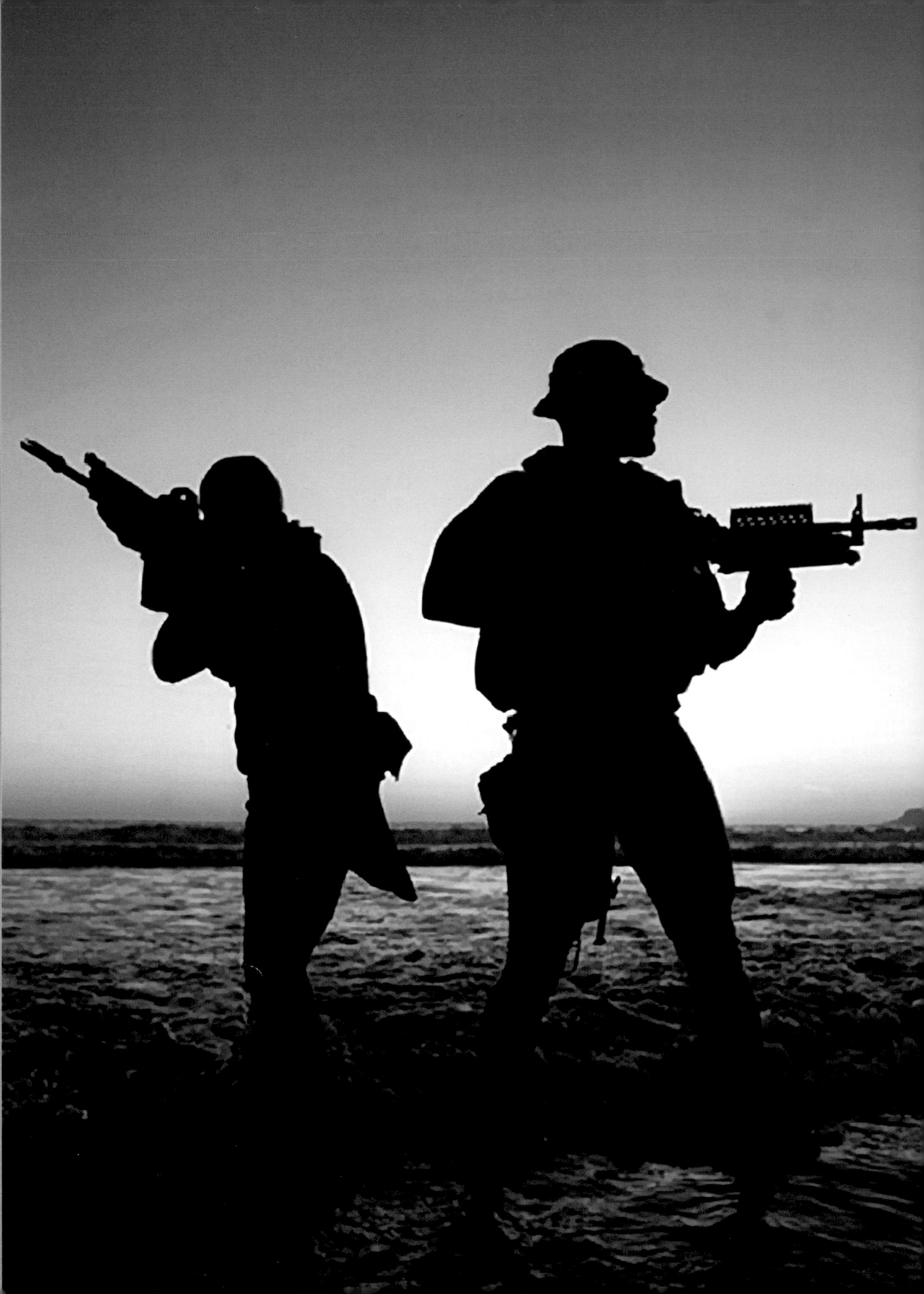

FIREPOWER AND FILMS

Because SEALs need to perform their missions with what they can carry with them into battle, they require light-weight weapons that provide a great deal of firepower. The primary weapon is the Colt M4A1 carbine, a shorter version of the M16A2 rifle, the weapon used by many conventional units in the U.S. armed forces. Its overall length is 33 inches (84 cm), with a 14.5-inch (37 cm) barrel. Fully loaded, it weighs about 6.5 pounds (3 kg). It can be fitted with accessories such as day- and night-vision scopes and the M203 grenade launcher. A particularly lethal addition is the "Masterkey," a modified Remington M870 12-gauge shotgun that mounts under the barrel. The Masterkey can fire either specially de-signed breaching rounds to blast off door hinges or standard shotgun ammunition to aid in clearing a room.

Many SEALs also carry the H&K MP5, which is six inches (15 cm) shorter than the M4. There is considerable evidence that SEAL Team Six members on the bin Laden raid carried the H&K MP7, which, at 25 inches (64 cm) in length and weighing just 2.7 pounds (1.2 km) is ideal for CQC. Its extendable stock and folding *foregrip* make it compact enough to be concealed under civilian clothes, which SEAL operators sometimes wear during their missions. All three weapons are often fitted with sound suppressors, which also reduce the amount of recoil.

Weapons have to withstand water, sand, and mud as SEALs transition between environments.

The most important backup weapon for SEALs is the Sig Sauer M11 9-mm pistol. At times, it can become their primary armament, especially in CQC situations such as capturing prisoners or rescuing hostages. The men reportedly like it for its compact size, its accuracy, and its durability. The M9 Beretta is another valuable sidearm.

SEALs rely on canine companions to find explosives and perform other sensitive tasks. The most common breed is the Belgian Malinois. Weighing about 65 pounds (30 kg), the animals can even parachute into action. They wear protective body armor and sometimes self-inflating life jackets. Equipped with video gear mounted on their heads, the animals can enter potential danger zones and beam back images of what they encounter.

All SOFs require a mode of transportation. SEALs often arrive via helicopter. Larger groups use the CH-47 Chinook, while smaller ones ride in choppers such as the UH-60 Black Hawk. SEALs are also highly skilled at jumping out of airplanes, sometimes from as high as six miles (9.6 km) above the earth where enemies can't hear or see the aircraft. There are several methods of coming in undetected from the sea. For example, the SEAL Delivery Vehicle (SDV) can carry up to four fully armed men and run for several hours on its batteries. It is 22 feet (6.7 m) long and weighs about 4 tons (3.6 t). Its two-man crew can "park" the vehicle on the bottom of the sea and join the attack. Modified attack or former ballistic missile submarines bring SDVs and SEAL personnel to locations close to attack sites. Some men go ashore on the SDVs, while others swim to the surface, inflate rubber rafts, and paddle silently to their objective.

All this firepower and a longstanding reputation for risk-taking have made SEALs popular subjects in the media. Former SEAL Dick Couch used his experiences in Vietnam to write his first novel, *Seal Team One*, in 1991. Two years later, he followed up with *Pressure Point*, in which terrorists take over a Washington

Before swimming across a frigid creek, SEALs pull on protective gloves and hoods.

State ferryboat and use it to hijack an American nuclear submarine armed with long-range nuclear missiles. Both books—and their successors—have been praised for their authenticity in depicting how SEALs carry out their missions.

Romance author Suzanne Brockmann became fascinated with SEALs and has written two series about fictitious units. "Troubleshooters, Inc." details the exploits of SEAL Team 16, while "Tall, Dark & Dangerous" deals with SEAL Team 10. "I took what I knew from my research and reading about Navy SEALs," Brockmann explains. "After I read as much as I possibly could, I began to sketch out my ideas." She became intrigued by their covert methods and stealthy ways and could easily imagine situations in which the operators would not want to "go in with their guns blazing."

SEAL Team Six founder Richard Marcinko has written more than a dozen action novels in the series of "Rogue Warrior," which is also the title of his nonfiction *memoir*. The central character is Dick Marcinko, a fictionalized version of the author. According to a review of 2012's *Rogue Warrior: Task Force Blue*, "As usual for a Rogue Warrior yarn, this one is a gripping hard-boiled thriller bulked up with information on weapons, hardware, and the psychology of the warrior, all of which takes on the authority conferred by Marcinko's personal experience. *Task Force Blue* may not win any new fans for the salty tongued Marcinko, but it will please the dickens out of all the current ones." The Rogue Warrior books have even inspired a set of video games.

In 1995, Steven Seagal reprised his role as an ex-SEAL in Under Siege 2: Dark Territory.

SEALs have played prominent roles in movies. In 1992's *Under Siege*, action hero Steven Seagal plays Casey Ryback, a ship's cook who becomes involved in a plot to capture the battleship USS *Missouri* and sell its

Tomahawk missiles to foreign powers. Unbeknownst to the plotters, Seagal is a highly decorated former SEAL who was *demoted* after a botched mission. He uses his training to defeat the plotters and save the day.

Actress Demi Moore starred as Lieutenant Jordan O'Neil in 1997's *G.I. Jane*. O'Neil is selected to become the first woman to undergo training for a fictional force called the U.S. Navy Combined Reconnaissance Team. Closely modeled on the SEALs, the Reconnaissance Team uses many of the same training methods. After experiencing harassment for being a woman, O'Neil becomes part of a rescue mission in Libya and earns the respect of her male colleagues—as well as some movie reviewers. Owen Gleiberman of *Entertainment Weekly* notes, "The film says that if women and men are to be truly equal, they must embrace the outer limits of physical will in the exact same way. *G.I. Jane* has a timely topic, which it treats with more than a touch of wish fulfillment." The wish may have been fulfilled. The U.S. armed forces' ban on women serving in combat roles was lifted early in 2013. Admiral William McRaven, head of all U.S. SOFs, said

Demi Moore prepared for G.I. Jane by training with a real-life Navy SEAL.

that he supported the decision and would move to include women in the SEALs. "It's time to do this," he commented. And Sean Rayment of the British newspaper *The Telegraph* noted, "G.I. Jane, the fictional special forces commando immortalized by the actress Demi Moore, will become a reality in the United States armed forces."

With the attack on Osama bin Laden's compound in 2011 serving to increase awareness of the SEALs even more, three films came out the following year. *Act of Valor* is a fictionalized account of SEAL operations, based on several real-life missions. While most critics panned the film, there was little doubt that the action scenes were authentic. They were performed by real-life SEALs—who in effect served as their own stunt doubles. *Zero Dark Thirty*, on the other hand, was critically acclaimed and was nominated for five Oscars for its account of the bin Laden manhunt. While SEALs portrayed in the film were all actors, there is general agreement that the scenes of the actual raid were accurately depicted. Another film based on the same subject, *SEAL Team Six: The Raid on Osama bin Laden* (which also uses actors to play SEALs), was not so successful. One reviewer of the made-for-television film said that it "strays from established reporting and official disclosures surrounding the May 1 [sic] raid in a number of ways."

Two of the biggest names in Hollywood—actor Bradley Cooper and director Steven Spielberg—teamed up to produce the forthcoming *American Sniper*. The film is based on the life of former SEAL sniper Chris Kyle, who reportedly had more kills than anyone else in U.S. military history. Kyle was shot in 2013 by one of the many veterans he tried to help following his retirement from the navy.

The film Zero Dark Thirty *takes its title from military slang for pitch-black night.*

FORCE FACTS Retired Marine Corps captain and Hollywood military film consultant Dale Dye wrote *Code Word: Geronimo*, a graphic novel about the bin Laden raid.

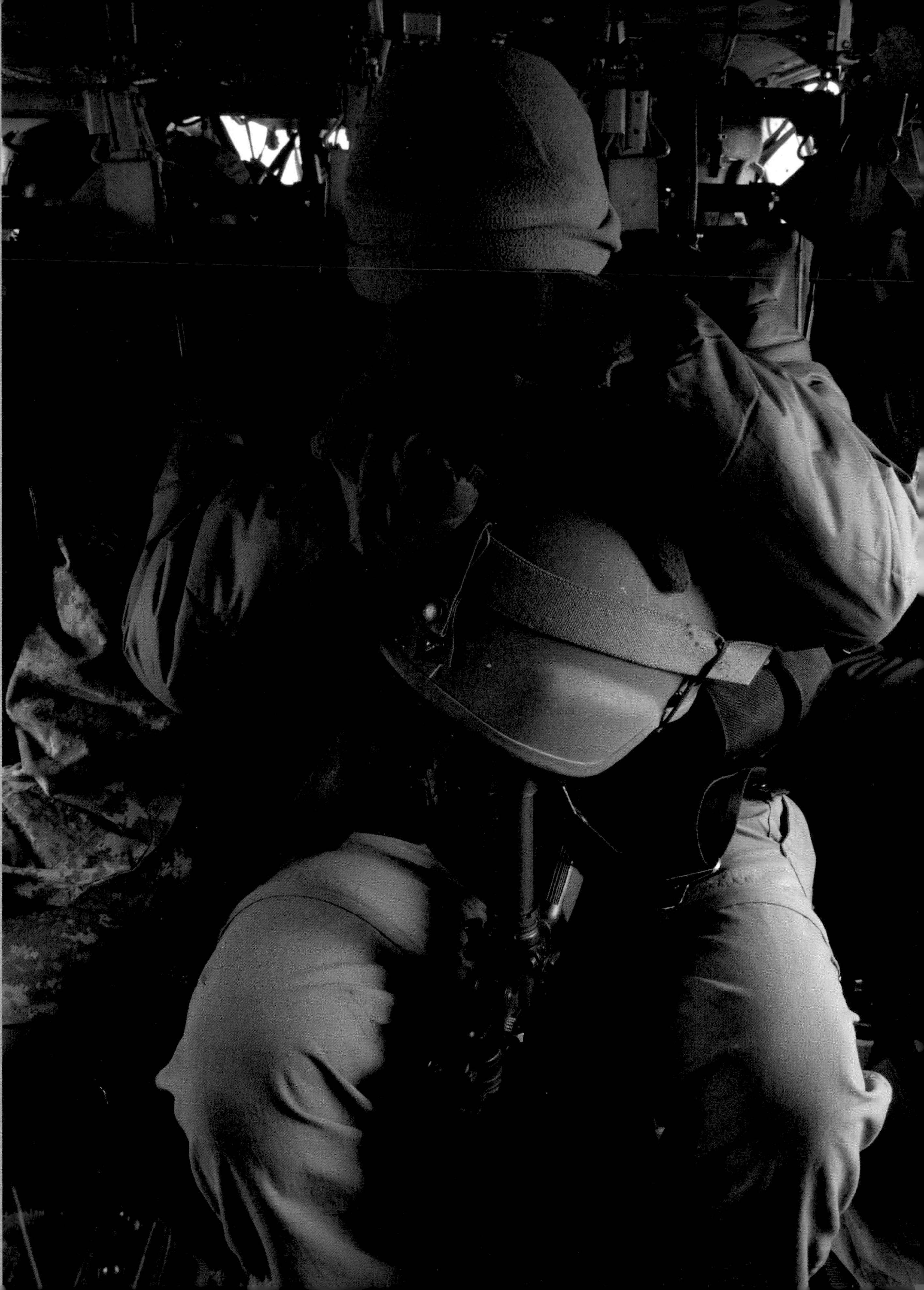

U.S. SPECIAL FORCES

SEALS IN ACTION

AS THE STRICKEN HELICOPTER CARRYING PART OF THE SEAL team that was about to attack Osama bin Laden's compound slammed into the ground, President Obama and the rest of his security team—who were in real-time contact with the mission—drew in their breaths. But the pilot landed in such a way that the aircraft wouldn't tip over and kill or seriously injure the SEALs inside. The men quickly poured out and linked up with the SEALs from the other helicopter. Moments later, the mission began in earnest, as the men used explosives to blow down doors and walls. It was completely dark because their partners from the Central Intelligence Agency (CIA) had cut the power from a remote site.

Suddenly, a man opened fire on the SEALs, but his aim was wild. The SEALs quickly shot him. Two other men were also gunned down. So was a woman used as a human shield by one of the gunmen. With the resistance overcome, the SEALs went room by room through the house.

While there is some controversy about the exact sequence of events, according to the most widely accepted source, bin Laden suddenly appeared on an upper floor. He rushed back to his room, where he had two weapons. But he never got to use them, as SEALs in hot pursuit shot him. Moments later, the team leader radioed, referring to the code name for bin Laden, "For God and country—Geronimo, Geronimo, Geronimo." Moments

SEALs flying toward a mission—even the bin Laden raid—use the time to rest and get ready.

FORCE FACTS SEAL operations take place all around the globe, from searching for drug smugglers in Bolivia to locating war criminals in Bosnia.

later he added, "Geronimo EKIA," meaning that bin Laden had been killed in action. With bin Laden dead, the SEALs scooped up computers and documents that could contain valuable information. Planners had estimated that the raid would take 40 minutes, and it was a tribute to the professionalism of the SEALs that it had actually taken only 38. The damaged helicopter was blown up, and a reserve helicopter flew in to retrieve the men and bin Laden's body. The body was flown to the aircraft carrier USS *Carl Vinson*. After performing appropriate Muslim religious rites, it was buried at sea. By then, President Obama had reported the news of the successful attack to the American people. Spontaneous celebrations erupted all across the nation.

Before the bin Laden raid, perhaps the highest-profile recent action involving SEALs came when Somali pirates boarded the U.S. merchant ship *Maersk Alabama* in the Indian Ocean on April 8, 2009. Most of the crew retreated to a secure place on the ship. Taking Captain Richard Phillips with them, the pirates tried to flee, using one of the ship's covered lifeboats. The destroyer USS *Bainbridge*—soon joined by other American warships—responded to the situation, isolated the lifeboat, and began towing it. Hostage negotiators from the Federal Bureau of Investigation (FBI) flew in but were unsuccessful in freeing the captain. Under cover of night, a number of SEALs parachuted into the sea and boarded the *Bainbridge*. Snipers positioned themselves near the ship's stern. As dusk fell four days after the incident began, two pirates stuck their heads out of a hatch. Moments later, the third appeared in a window and seemed as if he was about to shoot Phillips. The snipers fired simultaneously, with each one striking his target in the head. Phillips was saved.

One of the most notable early SEAL operations came in October 1972 during the final stages of American involvement in the Vietnam War. Known as Bat 21 Bravo, it began when an American aircraft was shot down in the midst of nearly 30,000

Combat divers perform high altitude–low opening (HALO) jumps from a C-130 Hercules.

FORCE FACTS When he was a SEAL in Vietnam, Bob Kerrey won the Medal of Honor and lost a foot. He later served Nebraska as governor (1983–87) and senator (1989–2001).

North Vietnamese soldiers. The surviving crewman, Lieutenant Colonel Iceal Hambleton, knew a great deal of secret information about U.S. missile forces and their targets. It was vital to keep him from falling into enemy hands, where he could give up this information under torture. Several air rescue missions failed during the next week, with the loss of more than 10 men and numerous aircraft. One would-be rescuer, Lieutenant Mark Clark, was among those shot down. Now there were two men in danger.

It became obvious that an air *extraction* wouldn't work. SEAL Lieutenant Thomas Norris, who had nearly washed out of BUD/S because of vision problems, assumed responsibility for the rescue. Leading five Vietnamese commandos upriver from a *forward operating base*, Norris evaded the North Vietnamese, found Clark, and brought him to safety. When a mortar attack killed two of his team members, two others became too frightened to continue. Norris and the remaining commando, Nguyen Van Kiet, penetrated nearly two miles (3.2 km) into enemy territory disguised as fishermen. They found Hambleton, who had suffered a broken wrist and lost 45 pounds (20 km) during his ordeal. As they paddled downriver, the North Vietnamese discovered them and laid down a heavy curtain of fire. The three men were unhurt, and Hambleton was evacuated. Norris would later receive the Medal of Honor for his heroism during the mission.

Six months after the Hambleton rescue, Norris, along with SEAL Petty Officer Mike Thornton, and three Vietnamese, came ashore in a rubber boat to conduct an intelligence-gathering mission in enemy-controlled territory. As they returned to their concealed boat several hours later, they came under heavy fire from dozens of enemy troops.

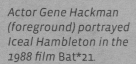

Actor Gene Hackman (foreground) portrayed Iceal Hambleton in the 1988 film Bat*21.

Thornton was hit in both legs and his back. Norris told him and two Vietnamese to return to the boat while he and the third Vietnamese covered them. A few moments later, Norris slumped to the ground with a head wound. The man with him fled to the relative safety of the boat.

"Where's my lieutenant?" Thornton demanded.

"Dead!" the Vietnamese man screamed. He urged the group to push off into the water immediately.

Thornton shook his head. "Not without my lieutenant."

Despite his wounds, Thornton rushed back to Norris. He shot two enemy soldiers who arrived at the same time, threw Norris over his shoulder, and—miraculously—escaped the heavy enemy fire as he dashed into the water. Thornton inflated their life preservers, and two hours later they were picked up. Norris survived, and Thornton was awarded the Medal of Honor in 1973.

SEALs have been an essential element in the Middle East for more than two decades. One of their first missions came soon after then Iraqi dictator Saddam Hussein invaded Kuwait in August 1990. Several months later, a U.S.-led *coalition* was ready to

After arriving in Vietnam, camouflaged SEALs earned the nickname "men with green faces."

move into Kuwait. At first, coalition leaders considered a traditional *amphibious operation*, but the idea was rejected in favor of a land offensive. Even then, the cost in coalition lives could be high. So it became necessary to convince the Iraqis that they were facing a seaborne assault and tie down a significant portion of their heavy armor far from the site of the actual attack.

After discovering a suitable site for the would-be "invasion," the SEALs paddled ashore in the middle of the night and laid down explosive charges that were set to detonate several hours later. Speedboats zoomed in after them, throwing out orange buoys to mark the supposed landing zone. The deception worked. The land invasion encountered significantly less opposition than planners had feared.

Early in December 2012, members of the *Taliban* kidnapped an American physician and two Afghan medical workers who were on their way to a clinic. The Afghans were released several days later, but sources revealed that the physician was being beaten by his captors. Even worse, there were indications that the Taliban was planning on slipping across the border into Pakistan with him, making a rescue almost impossible. A SEAL Team Six unit was ordered to rescue the doctor. While few details are known, the team managed to save him while killing several members of the Taliban and arresting two of its leaders. Unfortunately, Petty Officer 1st Class Nicolas D. Checque, a SEAL for several years, was killed. "In this fallen hero, and all of our special operators, Americans see the highest ideals of citizenship, sacrifice, and service upheld," said U.S. defense secretary Leon Panetta. "The torch of freedom burns brighter because of them."

Or as special forces expert Fred Pushies notes, a SEAL team member gave him a T-shirt that read, "To find us, you've got to be smart. To catch us, you've got to be fast. To beat us, you've got to be kidding!" Such unwavering confidence and the ability to back it up with real skill will be needed in the years ahead. The SEALs have many enemies to beat.

Jon Tumilson and 37 others were killed when their helicopter was shot down in Afghanistan.

★ ★ ★

FORCE FACTS At the funeral of SEAL Jon Tumilson in August 2011, his dog Hawkeye lay next to the casket during the service. A friend of Tumilson's later adopted Hawkeye.

BUD/S students practice
night-diving techniques
using masks that have
been blackened.

FORCE FACTS To gain confidence in the water during training, prospective SEALs have their hands and feet tied and then bob up and down in a swimming pool.

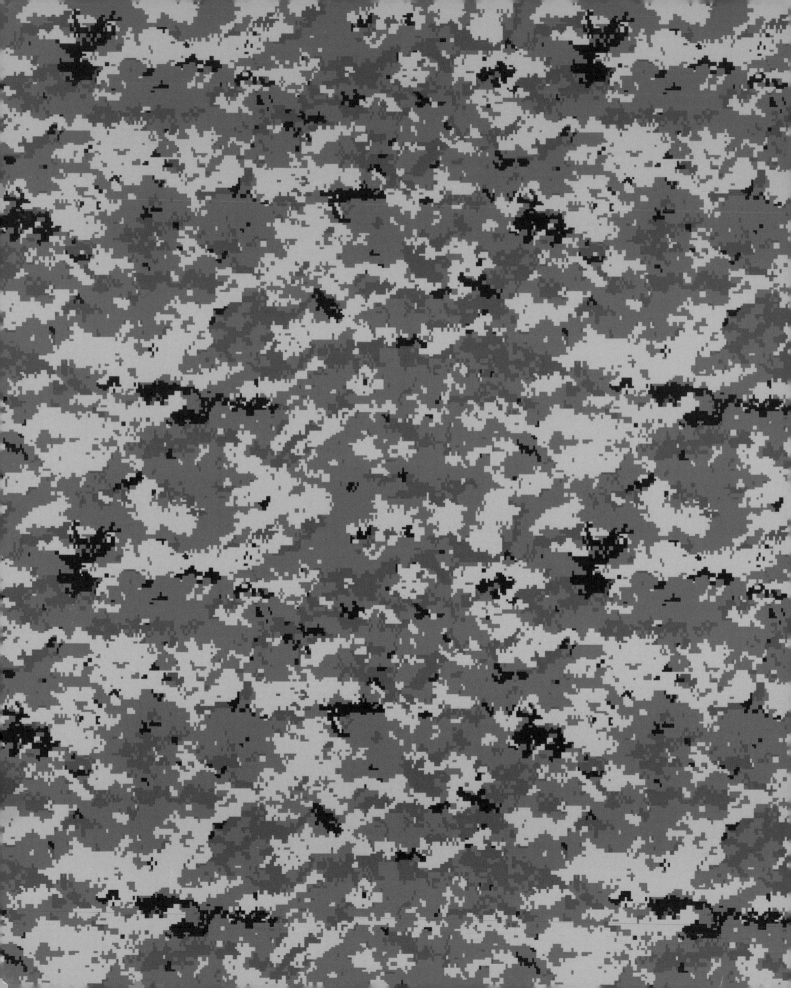

GLOSSARY

acronym – a word formed from the first letter or letters of other words

Allied – describing the combination of forces from the U.S., British Commonwealth, Soviet Union, and other countries that opposed the Axis powers of Germany, Japan, and Italy during World War II

amphibious operation – an assault from the sea that involves coordination of naval, airborne, and infantry components; it is generally regarded as the most complex and potentially riskiest of all military maneuvers

cadets – students training at a military school; naval cadets are called midshipmen

coalition – a temporary alliance to undertake a combined action

Crusades – organized military efforts conducted by Christian forces to reclaim the Holy Land from the Muslims in the 11th, 12th, and 13th centuries

demoted – reduced in rank

deployment – movement of personnel into position for military action

downwash – downward air turbulence caused by a helicopter rotor

enlisted men – those who sign up voluntarily for military duty at a rank below an officer; they compose the largest part of military units

extraction – a safe withdrawal from a mission

foregrip – the handle of a weapon mounted under the front part of the barrel

forward operating base – a base established in friendly territory near enemy lines to provide support for tactical operations

guerrilla – a fighter who isn't part of conventional armed forces

hypothermic – having abnormally low body temperature

indoctrination – instruction in a set of basic principles or ideas

memoir – a personal account based on the subject's experiences and memories

reconnaissance – a search to gain information, usually conducted in secret

romance – a type of literature dealing with love in a sentimental way

small-unit tactics – techniques of dealing with combat situations for platoons and smaller units

Taliban – a fundamentalist Islamic political movement and militia that controlled Afghanistan; noted especially for terror tactics and a repressive attitude toward women

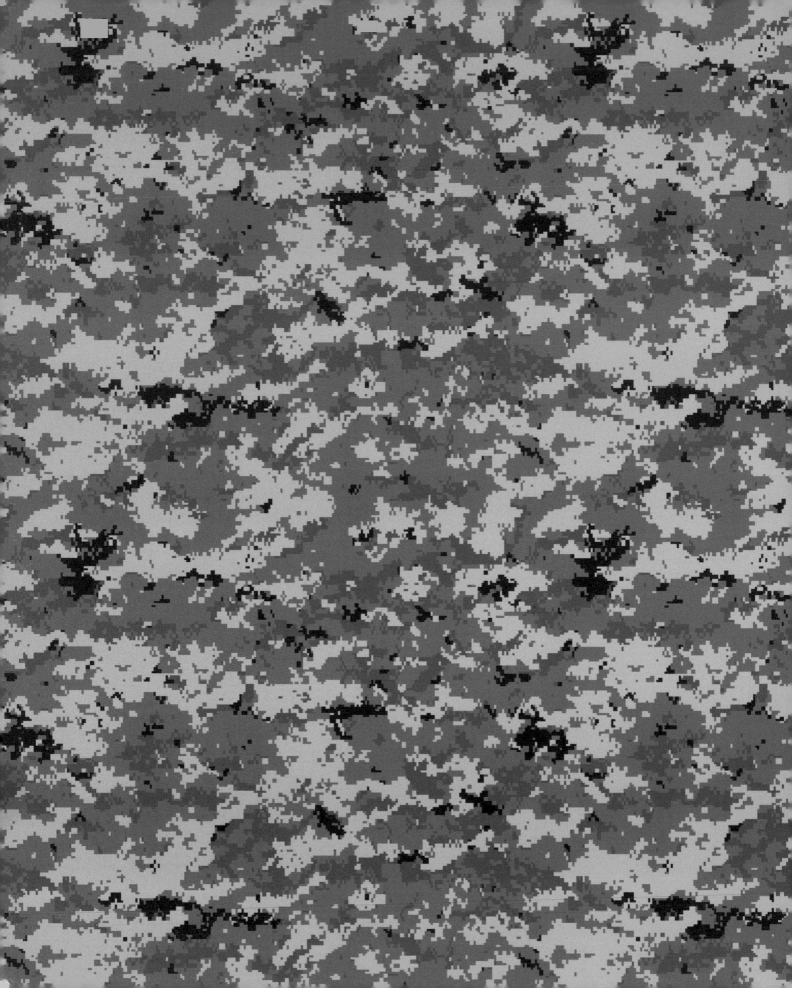

SELECTED BIBLIOGRAPHY

U.S. SPECIAL FORCES

Cantrell, Mark, and Donald Vaughan. *Special Forces: America's Elite*. Bonita Springs, Fla.: The Media Source, 2012.

Couch, Dick. *Down Range: Navy SEALs in the War on Terrorism*. New York: Crown, 2005.

Halberstadt, Hans. *U.S. Navy SEALs in Action*. St. Paul, Minn.: MBI Publishing, 1995.

Marcinko, Richard, with John Weisman. *Rogue Warrior*. New York: Pocket Books, 1992.

Owen, Mark, with Kevin Maurer. *No Easy Day: The Autobiography of a Navy SEAL*. New York: Dutton, 2012.

Pushies, Fred. *Weapons of the Navy SEALs*. St. Paul, Minn.: MBI Publishing, 2004.

Tucker, David, and Christopher J. Lamb. *United States Special Operations Forces*. New York: Columbia University Press, 2007.

Wasdin, Howard, and Stephen Templin. *I Am a SEAL Team Six Warrior: Memoirs of an American Soldier*. New York: St. Martin's Griffin, 2012.

WEBSITES

Naval Special Warfare

http://www.americanspecialops.com/navy-sof/

Find detailed information about SEALs and SEAL Team Six, including organization, equipment, notable operations, photos, videos, and more.

Navy SEALs

http://www.sealswcc.com/seal-default.aspx

The official SEALs website includes an overview, history, preparation for enlisting, training, videos, current news, and more.

READ MORE

Brush, Jim. *Special Forces*. Mankato, Minn.: Sea-to-Sea, 2012.

Cooper, Jason. *U.S. Special Operations*. Vero Beach, Fla.: Rourke, 2004.

Note: Every effort has been made to ensure that the websites listed above have educational value and that they contain no inappropriate material. However, because of the nature of the Internet, it is impossible to guarantee that these sites will remain active indefinitely or that their contents will not be altered.

INDEX